The Ultimate Self-Teaching Method! BEGINNER'S PACK

Play Violin Today!

A Complete Guide to the Basics

by Sharon Stosur

Violin by Jerry Loughney

PLAYBACK+
Speed • Pitch • Balance • Loop

To access audio and video visit:
www.halleonard.com/mylibrary
Enter Code
3926-2522-2588-8477

ISBN 978-1-5400-5244-5

Visit Hal Leonard Online at
www.halleonard.com

Contact us:
Hal Leonard
7777 West Bluemound Road
Milwaukee, WI 53213
Email: info@halleonard.com

In Europe, contact:
Hal Leonard Europe Limited
42 Wigmore Street
Marylebone, London, W1U 2RN
Email: info@halleonardeurope.com

In Australia, contact:
Hal Leonard Australia Pty. Ltd.
4 Lentara Court
Cheltenham, Victoria, 3192 Australia
Email: info@halleonard.com.au

Introduction

Track 1

Welcome to *Play Violin Today!*—the series designed to prepare you for any style of violin playing, from classical to folk to country. Whatever your taste in music, *Play Violin Today!* will give you the start you need.

About the Audio & Video

It's easy and fun to play the violin, and the accompanying online audio will make your learning even more enjoyable, as we take you step by step through each lesson and play each song along with full accompaniment. Much like a real lesson, the best way to learn this material is to first read and practice on your own, then listen to the audio. With *Play Violin Today!*, you can learn at your own pace. If there is ever something you don't quite understand the first time through, go back to the audio and listen again. Every musical track has been given a number, so if you want to practice a song again, you can find it right away.

Some lessons in the book include video, so you can see and hear the material being taught. Audio and video are indicated with icons.

Audio Icon   Video Icon

Contents

Lesson 1 | The Basics

The Parts of the Violin

Track 2

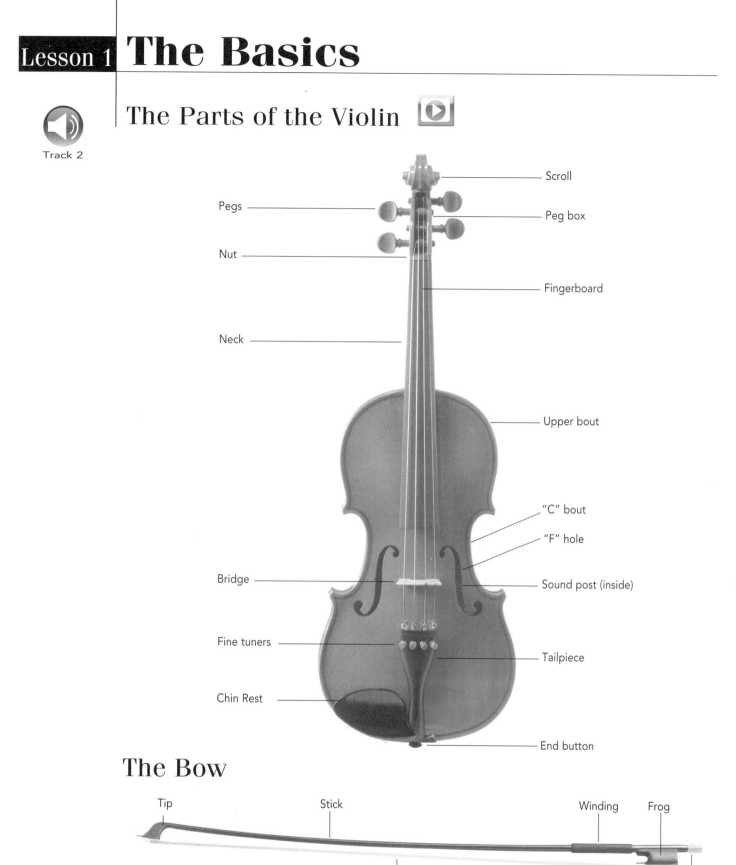

Scroll

Pegs

Peg box

Nut

Fingerboard

Neck

Upper bout

"C" bout

"F" hole

Bridge

Sound post (inside)

Fine tuners

Tailpiece

Chin Rest

End button

The Bow

Tip   Stick   Winding   Frog

Bow hair   Ferrule

Adjusting Screw

Accessories

You will also need rosin for your bow, and a soft cloth for removing fingerprints and rosin dust before putting your violin back in the case. You may wish to use a shoulder rest to help hold the violin more comfortably. Shoulder rests attach to the underside of your violin and can be purchased at your local music store, available in a variety of materials and styles. Some string players use a soft sponge or cloth in place of the shoulder rest. A shoulder rest is not required to hold the violin properly, but many players find them to be helpful. You may wish to experiment with several types to decide what works best for you.

3

Holding Your Violin

With the left hand, pick up your violin by the neck with the strings facing away from you. Hold the instrument where the neck meets the body. If you grab it too close to the pegs, you may "bump" them, throwing the instrument out of tune.

Turn the violin toward you, with the strings facing the ceiling. Bring the violin to your left shoulder placing the side of your left jaw against the chin rest, creating a slight angle between your face and the violin, with the violin angling to the left.

Although it is called a chin rest, your chin never rests directly on the chin rest, rather your jaw is what comes most in contact with it. Slide your right hand toward the pegs, stopping about 1 1/2 inches in front of the nut. Curve your fingers slightly around the neck to touch the strings. Your thumb remains unbent, resting against the left side of the neck. Your left hand cradles the neck in this way, however it does not support the weight of your instrument. Your shoulder and chin support and hold the instrument. Your left wrist should be straight, and your left arm and elbow should be directly beneath the middle of the violin. Practice holding the violin under your chin without your left hand for several seconds, gradually adding to the amount of time you can support the violin

without your left hand. Try to keep your neck and shoulder as relaxed as possible while still supporting the weight of the violin. You may find that a soft sponge or shoulder rest attached beneath the violin will help cushion the space between the violin and your shoulder. This can help make holding the violin more comfortable.

The Bow

Preparing Your Bow

When a bow is stored in its case, the hair is loosened. After taking the bow from your case to play, you will need to tighten the hair by turning the screw clockwise, until the hair is straight and firm, still leaving the stick visibly bowed. Take care not to over tighten the hair, which could damage the bow and produce a harsh sound.

Before playing, rosin the bow by holding the rosin in your left hand while sliding the bow back and forth across the rosin, moving the bow and holding the rosin steady. You will need to apply a little rosin each time you take your violin out to play.

Remember to loosen the bow hair by turning the screw counterclockwise before putting the bow back in the case again.

Holding the Bow

As you learn to hold the bow for the first time, put down your violin so your left hand can assist you. As you become more comfortable with your bow, you will be able to pick it up easily with your right hand alone.

Using your left hand, pick up the bow in the middle of the stick with the hair facing the floor. You should always avoid touching the hair. Place the tip of your right thumb against the spot where the left end of the frog meets the stick, bending your thumb joint slightly.

Allow your middle and ring fingers to curve over the stick—your middle finger roughly opposite your thumb, touching the ferrule. The first joint of your index finger will rest along the top of the stick in the middle of the winding, and the tip of your little finger will rest on top of the stick near the screw. Your hand should be relaxed with the fingers spread comfortably. You will want to practice finding this position several times each day until it becomes easy.

The hair should still be facing the floor. Carefully let go of the stick with your left hand. You will notice the weighty feeling on the frog side of the bow.

Learning to properly hold the bow takes a little patience and practice. As you begin to learn notes on the violin, you may wish to pluck the string first, instead of using the bow right away. Plucking a stringed instrument is called "pizzicato." As you play new notes and pieces pizzicato, continue to practice holding the bow to become more comfortable with it.

Track 6

Tuning Your Violin

The four strings on the violin are tuned to the following pitches,
from bottom (low) to top (high): G, D, A, E.

You can adjust each pitch by tightening or loosening each string by turning its corresponding peg.
You can make very small adjustments to the string by turning the fine tuners. To tune your violin
it is easiest to use an electronic tuner or a piano or keyboard. You may also use a pitch pipe or
tuning fork. The online audio will also enable you to tune your violin. Listen to each pitch, starting
with the highest, and adjust the strings as necessary to match the pitches. Always tune your
instrument before playing.

Violin Care Tip

When placing the violin back in its case, always wipe the rosin off the strings with a soft cloth. This will
ensure a longer string life. Also, to protect the wood of the instrument, it is good to place a humidifier
in the case during the colder months of the year. Ask for a violin humidifier at your local music store.

Track 7

Tuning the E String:

Rest your violin on your knees with the strings facing you. Listen to the E on audio, electric tuner, or
piano. Pluck the E on your violin to determine if it matches the E being played. Raise the pitch by
turning the corresponding peg slowly and carefully *away* from you. Lower the pitch by turning the
peg slowly and carefully *toward* you. If the pitch is very close, use the fine tuner to a make a smaller
adjustment. (Not all violins come equipped with fine tuners on all four strings. As a beginner, it is
recommended you have a fine tuner on each string.) Turning the fine tuner clockwise **raises** the pitch,
counterclockwise **lowers** the pitch. Continue tuning the other three strings in the same manner.

Some Tuning Tips:

While tightening or loosening a string, turn the peg or fine tuner slowly, concentrating on the
changes in pitch. You might need to pluck the string repeatedly to compare the sound of your string
to the note you are tuning to.

As you're tuning a string, you may notice a series of pulsating beat waves. These beat waves can
help you tune; they'll slow down as the pitches get closer together, stopping completely when the
two pitches are the same, meaning they are in tune.

Instead of tuning a string down to a pitch, tune it up. This allows you to stretch the string into place,
which will help it stay in tune longer. If a string is too high in pitch, tune it down first, then bring it
back up to pitch. Always be careful not to tune a string too high or too quickly. Strings can break
easily as a result, especially the E string.

Reading Music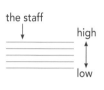

Musical sounds are indicated by symbols called **notes**. The two most important components to every note are **pitch** and **rhythm**.

Pitch

Pitch (the highness or lowness of a note) is indicated by the horizontal placement of a note on the staff. Notes higher on the staff are higher in pitch. To name the pitches, we use the first seven letters of the alphabet: A, B, C, D, E, F, and G. The treble clef ♣** assigns a particular pitch name to each line and space on the staff, centered around the pitch G, located on the second line from the bottom. Music for violin is always written in the treble clef. (Depending on range, some instruments use other clefs. The cello, for example, a lower sounding instrument, uses the bass clef.)

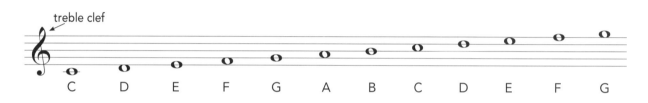

An easy way to remember the pitches on the lines is "**E**very **G**ood **B**oy **D**oes **F**ine." For the spaces, spell "FACE."

Rhythm

Rhythm refers to the elements of time—how long, or for how many beats a note lasts, including spaces or rests in between notes. Notes of different durations are represented by the following symbols:

To help you keep track of beats in a piece of music, the staff is divided into measures (or "bars"). A time signature (or "meter") at the beginning of the staff indicates how many beats you can expect to find in each measure.

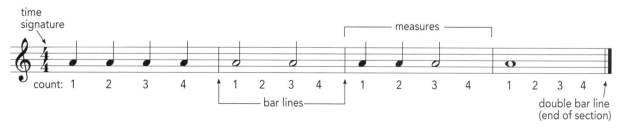

4/4 is perhaps the most common time signature. The top number indicates how many beats there are in each measure. The bottom number shows what kind of note value receives one beat ("4" is most often on the bottom, but numbers such as "8" or even "2" are used as well). In 4/4 time, there are four beats in each measure, and each beat is worth one quarter note.

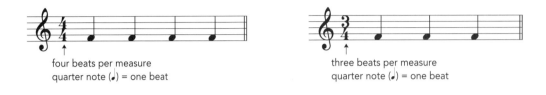

four beats per measure
quarter note (♩) = one beat

three beats per measure
quarter note (♩) = one beat

Accidentals

Any note can be raised or lowered a half step by placing an **accidental** directly before it.

Sharp (♯) ⟶ Raises a note one half step

Flat (♭) ⟶ Lowers a note one half step

Natural (♮) ⟶ Cancels previously used sharp or flat

Open Strings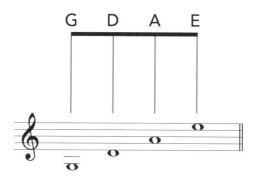

Track 8

From lowest to highest, the strings on the violin are: G D A E.

Memorize the names of the strings and their corresponding notes on the staff by playing the notes *pizzicato* (plucked, often abbreviated as *pizz.*). With your violin in proper position on your left shoulder, place your right thumb against the lower right hand corner of the fingerboard under the E string. Use your index finger to pluck each of the open strings. A gentle but firm plucking motion will produce a good tone.

Pizzicato vs. Arco

Usually, when no instruction is given as to whether or not the tune should be plucked or bowed, it is assumed that bowing will be used. The term **arco** (with the bow) is usually used to instruct the player to start using the bow after a passage that was just played **pizzicato**.

Note Names

Say the names of the open strings aloud as you play "Open String Pizzicato" and "Open String Challenge." Doing so will help you learn the letter names on the staff faster. Feel free to sing them as well.

Track 9

Open String Pizzicato

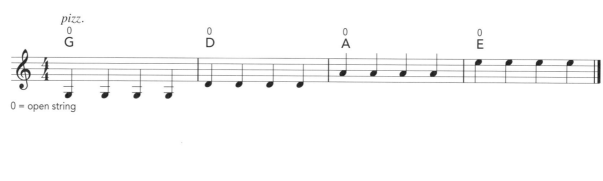

0 = open string

► If you pluck too hard, the string will snap back against the fingerboard producing a loud, percussive sound (snap pizz.).

Open String Challenge

Track 10

Placing the Bow on the Strings

Hold your violin in its proper position with your left hand, and your bow in your right hand. Place the hair of the bow, starting near the frog, on the D string, about halfway between the bridge and the end of the fingerboard (slightly closer to the brige). Your bow arm should be bent at about a 90 degree angle. Draw the bow across the string, opening your arm from the elbow in a downward motion toward the floor. This is called "down bow." Use enough weight on the string to create a ringing tone.

Now close your arm from the elbow bringing the bow back across the string, moving the bow toward you in an upward, or opposite motion. This is called "up bow." Practice bowing each open string to become comfortable with the down bow and up bow motions. If you become tense or tired while practicing, stop and rest a few moments before you resume.

⊓ = **down bow**: drawing the bow downward, towards the floor

V = **up bow**: drawing the bow upward, towards you

Bowing on Open Strings

As you play "Open String Bowing," use a down bow for the first half note in each measure, and an up bow for the second half note in each measure. When you see the indication *arco* in the music, it means to play with the bow on the string.

Open String Bowing

Track 11

Raise and lower your arm slightly as you move from string to string. Keep your bow halfway between the bridge and the end of the fingerboard. If you find your bow creeping down toward the bridge, slow down.

More Open Strings

Practice check list:

- Proper violin position
- Relaxed bow hold
- Bow placed halfway between bridge and fingerboard
- Slight arm shift from string to string
- Steady quarter-note beat

"Open String Warm Up" can be used as a daily warm up. Play it *pizzicato* first, and then use your bow.

Open String Warm Up

Notes on the D String

New Note: E

The note E sounds a whole step above the open D string. Place your first finger on the D string about 1 1/4 inches below the nut to sound the note E. Your nail should be facing you. Keep your other fingers curved over the strings but not touching the strings, being careful not to let the little finger curl under the fingerboard.

E

Whole Steps and Half Steps

Whole step: two half steps, or the distance between two white keys (with a black key in between) on a piano keyboard. The first three notes of a major scale (do-re-mi) are whole steps.

Half Step: the smallest distance in traditional music, or the distance from one white key to the closest possible key (black or white), with no keys in between, on the keyboard.

First Finger on D String

As you play "Aiming for E" (pizzicato), concentrate on the sound of the whole step between open D string and first finger E. Determine exactly where your first finger should be placed to sound a whole step higher.

Aiming for E

Track 17

New Note: F♯

A sharp symbol (♯) raises a note a half step. Placing a sharp on the staff before F raises the note, making it F sharp. F♯ sounds a whole step higher than first finger E. To play F♯, place your second finger about one inch from the first finger, keeping your first finger on E.

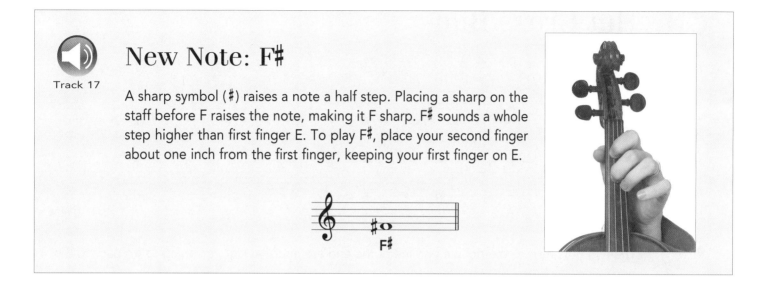

Memorize where the first and second fingers are placed to sound the E and F♯. Use your ear and the online audio to help check your **intonation** (accuracy of pitch). The first three notes are a whole step apart, like "do-re-mi."

Track 18

Second Finger on D String

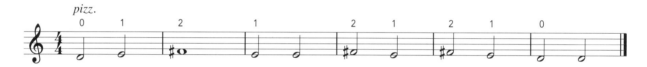

As you play "Putting It All Together," pluck the notes slowly, concentrating on finger placement and intonation. Gradually play faster as you get more comfortable. When the notes become easy, use the bowings given, but again, start slowly at first. Notice that in the fourth measure, we go from D up to F♯, skipping E. When playing the F♯, both fingers 1 and 2 will go down at the same time.

Track 19

Putting It All Together

Once you are comfortable playing both *pizz.* and *arco* on this song, go back in the book and try playing the earlier songs *arco*.

Hot Cross Buns

► Now, you must play *pizz.* while holding the bow so it is ready for *arco* when you repeat. Curve your hand around the frog, still using the index finger to pluck.

The two dots next to the double bar line at the end are a repeat sign, meaning to go back to the beginning.

Rests

Rests indicate beats of silence.

Quarter Rest = 1 beat of silence—the same duration as a quarter note.

Half Rest = 2 beats of silence—the same duration as a half note.

Whole Rest = 4 beats of silence—the same duration as a whole note, or simply resting for a whole measure.

| quarter rest (one beat) | half rest (two beats) | whole rest (four beats) or whole measure |

In "Mary's Lamb," use the rests in measures 2, 3, and 4 to lift and move the bow to again play down bow on beat one of the next measure.

Mary's Lamb

14

Lesson 4 Notes on the A String

As we move over to the A string to learn some new notes, use "Open String Review" to refresh your memory on the note names. You may also use this as an opportunity to practice slightly lowering and raising your bow arm as you move from string to string to play each one clearly.

Track 22

Open String Review

1st time pizz.
2nd time arco

Track 23

New Note: B

First Finger on the A String: B – The note B sounds a whole step higher than open A string. Place your finger about 1 1/4 inches below the nut to sound the note B on the A string, in about the same place as you placed first finger on the D string in the last lesson.

B

Track 24

Whole Step Happiness

pizz.

Track 25

Whole Step Hoedown

pizz.

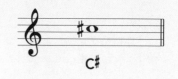
Track 26

New Note: C#

Second Finger on the A String: C# – The note C# sounds a whole step higher than first finger B. Place your second finger on the A string about one inch from the first finger, letting fingers 3 and 4 curve gently over the fingerboard. Remember to keep first finger down on the string while playing finger two.

C#

Putting It All Together on the A String

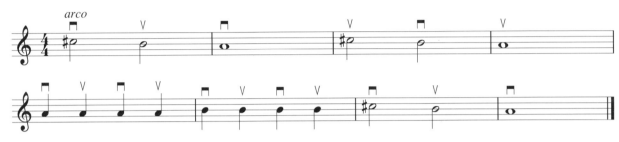

Remember playing "Hot Cross Buns" on the D string? Now try playing it on the A string. Remember to always tighten the bow hair and rosin your bow before playing. Take a minute to check for a relaxed bow hold.

Hot Cross Buns in A

Key Signature – D

A key signature indicates what notes to play sharp or flat throughout an entire piece. When sharps are indicated in a key signature, they are no longer placed next to each note on the staff. A key signature with two sharps indicates that all written Fs and Cs should be played as sharps. This is the **Key of D**.

Now try "French Folk Song" with your bow. Notice that each measure begins down bow. In measure 4, lift your bow during the half rest so you can begin measure 5 down bow.

French Folk Song

Lift and Breathe

The comma above the staff in "French Folk Song" is the sign to lift your bow. This is the same symbol used to tell wind instrument players to take a breath. This lift motion is also referred to as a *circle bow*, as you are making a circle in the air, returning the bow to the starting point for another down bow. As a string player, it is good to use these markings not only to lift the bow, but to breathe as well. Doing so helps promote a kind of natural phrasing to the song you are playing.

New Note on the D String: G

New Note: G

The note G sounds a half step higher than F#. This is a smaller **interval** than the whole steps you have been playing. To find the G on the D string, place finger three on the fingerboard right next to finger two. Fingers two and three should be slightly touching. Be sure that the fourth finger is curled over the fingerboard and not curled under.

G

As you are playing the next song, getting used to the new note G, practice slowly, playing *pizzicato*. Try playing it on your own, without the audio. When you are comfortable with it, play track 31 and try playing along.

New Note G Etude

Track 31

Intervals

An interval is the distance between two pitches. So far, we have discussed the intervals half step and whole step. Your violin is tuned by another interval, the fifth. From bottom to top, each string is a fifth apart: G (a b c) D (e f g) A (b c d) E. To find any interval, count, beginning with the first pitch as one, and stop at your desired pitch. This number is the interval. For example, A up to C is a third: A (1), B (2), C (3), = 3rd.

Practice "D String Etude" *pizzicato* first, without holding the bow. Next, play *pizz.* while holding the bow. After that, practice *arco*, and when you are ready, try going from *pizz.* to *arco* on the repeat, without stopping.

D String Etude

Track 32

By adding open string A to the notes you've learned on the D string, you can play a five-note **scale**. Keep finger 3 down on the D string as you play open A. This way you are ready to play finger 3 again, right away.

Track 33

Five Note Scale

Always listen to yourself as you play to make sure you are in tune. What is the interval between D and A in the last measure? The intervals in the first three measures are all steps, but which are half steps, and which are whole steps?

Scales

A *scale* is a series of ascending or descending notes, arranged sequentially (following the alphabet, in order). The type of scale is defined by the intervals between each scale degree, primarily determined by which are half steps **(H)** and which are whole steps **(W)**. For example, the arrangement of **W W H W W W H** is a **major scale**. If one begins on C, this scale would be all natural notes (no sharps or flats). To begin on D and follow this pattern would give us F sharp and C sharp. This D major scale is the basis for many of the tunes in this book.

"Bile 'em Cabbage" is a popular American fiddle tune. Keep a steady quarter-note beat using smooth longer bows for the half notes. The song is based on the notes of the D major scale. The entire D major scale will be introduced on page 21.

Track 34

Bile 'em Cabbage

"Jingle Bells" uses notes on the D string and the open A string. When you are ready to try "Jingle Bells" with your bow, notice you will be lifting when there is a rest on beat 4, as in measures 4 and 12. Practice this motion in the air before putting your bow on the string.

Jingle Bells

In this theme from Dvořák's "New World Symphony," notice the line marked under the notes in measures 1–2, 3, and 5–6. This is a reminder that after playing finger 2 on F♯, you should keep finger 2 on the D string while you play the open A, coming right back to the F♯. Also note that during the rest in measure 4, you will lift your bow to begin down bow in measure 5.

New World Symphony Theme

Antonín Dvořák

Lesson 6 — New Note on the A String: D

Track 37

New Note: D

The note D sounds a half step higher than C♯. To play a D on the A string, place your third finger on the A string right next to the second finger, with the second and third fingers slightly touching. This D is an **octave** higher than the open D string. Play open D and then D on the A string to compare the sound.

D

Play "High D–Low D" pizzicato, listening for the half step between C♯ and D, and the difference between the high and the low D.

High D–Low D

Track 38

A String Etude

·Track 39

Notice the time signature in "Melody." There are 3 beats in each measure. Use a longer bow stroke to give the dotted half note 3 full beats.

Melody

Track 40

20

Dynamics

Dynamics indicate how loud or soft the music will be played. Traditionally, dynamic terms are known by their Italian names:

p	*piano*	soft	*mp*	*mezzo piano*	moderately soft
f	*forte*	loud	*mf*	*mezzo forte*	moderately loud

Using a heavier bow stroke and a faster bow speed will create a louder tone. A slower bow speed and less weight on the bow will create a softer tone.

In "Aunt Rhody," note the change in dynamics. Start the piece with a strong bow stroke. In measure 7, use less weight for a softer sound.

Track 41

Aunt Rhody

Track 42

Playing the D Major Scale

You are now ready to play a D major scale. Starting with the open D string, play up to finger three, the note G. Continue, now starting on the open A string, going up to finger three, sounding the note D (an octave higher than where you started). Play the scale *pizzicato* with the audio to check for intonation. Play the scale *arco* when the fingering becomes easy. Next, try playing a descending scale—start with the high D and go down, playing the same notes you did on the way up.

Track 43

D Major Scale

Track 44

Double Up

21

Track 45

New Note: F#

The note F# sounds a whole step above open E string. Place your first finger on the E string about 1 1/4 inches below the nut to sound F#.

F#

Track 46

Effortless F#

▶ With this new key signature, only the Fs are sharp.

Only one sharp in the key signature: G major

Track 47

Whole Step Cha-Cha

Adding F# to the notes you are familiar with on the A string will enable you to play the following well-known folk tune.

Track 48

Twinkle

▶ With this new key signature, all Fs, Cs, and Gs are played as sharps.

Three sharps: key of A major

New Note: G#

Track 49

Second Finger on the E String: G# – This note sounds a whole step above first finger F#. Place your second finger on the E string about one inch from the first finger. Remember to keep fingers 3 and 4 curved over the fingerboard.

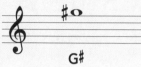

Whole Step Waltz

Track 50

"Hungarian Folk Song" uses notes on both the E and A strings. Play slowly at first, and when you are comfortable with the notes and rhythms, try a lively tempo.

Hungarian Folk Song

Track 51

Bartok

► Only the beginning down bow is given. Often a piece written mostly in quarter notes will use an alternating "down bow, up bow" pattern.

Long, Long Ago

Track 52

► Be sure that your fingering hand remains in a relaxed, curved position as you move between the A and E strings.

Notes on the G String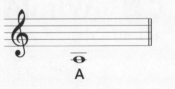

Track 53

New Note: A

The note A sounds a whole step higher than the open G string. Place your first finger on the G string about 1 ¼ inches below the nut to sound A. This A is one octave below the open string A. Remember to keep your fingers curved over the fingerboard.

A

Track 54

A New Note

Track 55

New Note: B

The note B sounds a whole step higher than A. Place your second finger on the G string, about one inch from the first finger to sound B.

B

As you play "March on the G String," listen for whole steps between open G, A, and B. Check the time signature. How many beats are in each measure?

March on the G String

Track 56

"G String Etude" uses notes on the G and D strings. Can you name all the notes?

G String Etude

Track 57

Tempo Marking

Tempo refers to the speed at which a piece of music is played. In music, tempo markings are often indicated in Italian. A few common tempo indications include:

Allegro: fast

Moderato: moderate

Andante: slower "walking" tempo

Largo: very slow

Upbeat

Also called a "*pick-up note*," an **upbeat** is a note or notes that appear before the first full measure. The remaining beats are found at the end of the song. Should there be a repeat sign at the end, the last measure, combined with the first measure make up one complete measure when repeating back to the beginning without stopping.

Oh Susannah

Track 58

The beautiful "Scottish Air," also known as "Annie Laurie," presents you with a new bowing challenge. Notice in measure two there are two up bows marked in a row. Use half of the bow for the half note, saving some bow to play the repeated E up bow on beat 4. This bowing pattern is also found in measures 6 and 14. Practice these measures separately to get a feel for this new bowing. Don't forget to begin the piece with an up bow on the first note.

Track 59

Scottish Air

► Many different intervals are used in this song. Can you name them? Remember to check your tuning on all intervals.

The Octave

You've already learned the intervals half step, whole step, and fifth. Another important interval makes an appearance in "Scottish Air." The **octave** is the distance from one letter name, to the nearest note of the same letter name, i.e., G to the next G, up or down. In "Scottish Air," octaves appear in measures 1, 5, and 15. Two notes an octave apart have a certain "sameness" in sound. Watch carefully for octaves in all songs, and make sure you play them in tune.

Lesson 9 | Playing in Close Position

Up until now you have played fingers one, two, and three in just about the same place on each string. As you worked on learning the notes in these positions, you have realized that *where* you put your finger on the string affects the pitch. In this lesson, the placement of finger two on the D and A strings will change, creating new notes.

Track 60

New Note: F

Close Position on the D String (low two): F (or "F natural," as opposed to F sharp).

To play F♮, which is only a half step higher than first finger E, place finger one to play an E and then place your second finger right next to the first finger. Fingers one and two should be slightly touching. This note is F♮. Some string players call this "low finger two," or two in "close" position, to distinguish it from finger two on the D string to play F♯ as you have previously learned. (F♮ is a half step lower than F sharp).

F

Natural Sign

A natural sign (♮) cancels a sharp or flat.

Track 61

Low 2 Blues

► The "2" with the arrow above indicates the "low 2" position.

Minor vs. Major

So far, we have learned about and played tunes in a major key. In general, major keys sound happy and bright. Minor keys sound sad and dark. Whether a tune is in major or minor depends largely on where the half steps are positioned in the scale.

Try "Low Aunt Rhody" by playing all the F♯s as F♮s, with finger two in close position. Try playing it again with finger two playing F♯. Can you hear the difference? Playing the F♯ puts "Aunt Rhody" in a major key, while playing F♮ changes "Aunt Rhody" to a minor key.

"Low" Aunt Rhody

► Does this sound like Aunt Rhody is sad? If so, you're doing well with the "low 2."

 Track 63

New Note: C

To play C (or C natural), place finger two in close position on the A string. Remember that fingers one and two should be slightly touching.

C

  Track 64

Close Friends

► Listen again to the sound of the half step between finger one and "low" finger two.

Track 65

German Folk Song

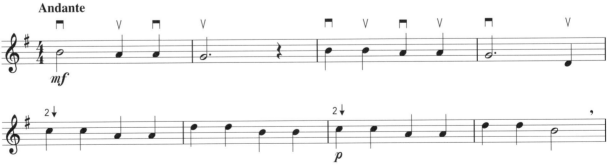

28

Can you find the C naturals in "Perfect Match?" Use a long bow stroke for the dotted half notes.

Track 66

Perfect Match

"Folk Song" uses low finger two on both the D and A strings. Notice the absence of sharps in the key signature. There are arrows indicating low finger two above the F naturals and C naturals to help you focus on finger placement.

Track 67

Folk Song

Are you ready for a challenge? "Bingo" uses C natural (low finger two on the A string) and F# (two on the D string).

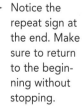

Track 68

Bingo

► Notice the repeat sign at the end. Make sure to return to the beginning without stopping.

Lesson 10 | Eighth Notes, Slurs, & Ties

Track 69

An *eighth note* sounds for one half the value of a quarter note. Eighth notes often appear in music in groups of two or four beamed together. Two eighth notes equal the value of one quarter note.

Counting and Tapping

You may wish to tap your foot to help keep time and play eighth notes evenly. If your foot taps on each quarter-note beat, then consider the act of your foot lifting up as "in between the beat." Quarter notes would be played once on each tap. Eighth notes would be played one on each tap, and one on each lift of the foot, in between the taps.

Play the D scale below using eighth-note rhythms. Set a quarter-note beat to determine the speed of your eighth notes. Use about half of the bow for each quarter note, and smaller bow strokes for each eighth note.

Track 70

Eighth Notes

Eighth notes can also be beamed in groups of 4 to make reading them easier.

Track 71

Lightly Row

30

Look for the eighth notes in measures 10–11 of "Ode to Joy." Set a steady quarter-note beat using full bow strokes for the half notes, half bows for the quarter notes, and even shorter bows for the eighth notes.

Ode to Joy

Track 72

Moderato

Beethoven

Slurs and Legato

String players often slur notes together, playing two or more notes with a single bow stroke. A **slur**, is a curved line connecting multiple notes, indicating this type of bowing.

Playing multiple notes in one bow stoke will cause the notes to sound smooth and connected. This style is known as **legato**.

Plenty to Slur

Track 73

▶ Listen for a smooth connected sound between the two slurred notes.

Andante

Observe the Music

A helpful tip to aid in learning any piece of music is to spend some time looking at the music before ever playing a note. Look for anything tricky that may come up such as large interval skips, changing dynamics, or even a change in key or meter. It is also useful to look for repeated patterns within the music. Some measures may look like something that occurred earlier, but in fact might be slightly different. Being aware of these similarities and differences will help you prepare to play the tune.

"Country Gardens" contains many repeated patterns. Identifying these will help you to learn the piece more quickly.

Country Gardens

Track 74

Practice Tips

"Caribbean Folk Song" is lively and fun to play. Some practice steps you may find useful include:

- Look at the music before playing, noticing every mark and symbol.
- Tap or clap the rhythm.
- Play *pizzicato* first to become familiar with the notes.
- Look ahead for slurs before bowing.

D.C. al Fine

D.C. stands for **Da Capo** which means "to the beginning." Fine means "end." When you see this sign, go back to the beginning of the song and play until Fine.

Caribbean Folk Song

Track 75

The Tie

As you look through "Amazing Grace" you will notice two types of curved lines above and below the notes. We already know the slur, but another type of curved line often used in music is called a tie. This looks like a slur, but connects two notes that are the same pitch. A tie between two notes makes the first note last the value of both notes tied together. Thus, a dotted half note (3 beats) tied to a half note (2 beats) will be held for 5 beats. Many ties are used to extend notes beyond the bar line. Move the bow more slowly to hold the note for a full 5 beats.

Track 76

Amazing Grace

► Be careful not to run out of bow when playing the long, tied notes.

"Theme from Brahms Symphony No. 1" contains several challenges. First, note the key signature: F will be played as F♯ throughout this piece. C will be C natural—low finger two on the A string. Notice that each pair of eighth notes is slurred. You might try bowing those measures in the air to get a feel for the bow pattern before playing. Also, carefully practice the two up bows in a row in measure 8. This theme is played in an easy, stately manner.

Track 77

Theme from Brahms Symphony No. 1

Crescendo and Decrescendo (or "Diminuendo")

These are two musical terms that indicate a gradual change in dynamics or "dynamic shading." Crescendo means to gradually get louder. Decrescendo means to gradually get softer. Symbols represent these terms to make it easy to see exactly where, and for how long the change in dynamics should occur.

crescendo (cresc.)

decrescendo (decresc. or dim.)

Practice crescendo and decrescendo as you play the following open-string exercises. Take some time with these exercises as you learn to adjust and create the sound you desire.

Track 78

Open String Crescendo

Track 79

Open String Decrescendo

A long-note crescendo will often be played with an up bow. Decrescendos are more easily executed with a down bow. Though this bowing is common, the reverse is still possible, and sometimes unavoidable.

Track 80

Open String Shading

Look ahead to see the crescendos and decrescendos in "Barbara Allen." Practice these measures separately until you achieve the sound you want. Also notice the single eighth note in the last measure. Count and tap this carefully.

Track 81

Barbara Allen

Scottish Folk Song

In "Scarborough Fair," words are used to indicate crescendo and diminuendo instead of symbols. Decide where the loudest point of the crescendo will be in measures 8–10. Practice these measures until your crescendo and decrescendo are smooth and easy.

Track 82

Scarborough Fair

English Folk Song

Two Duets

The next two pieces are duets. As you've played along with the audio so far, you were actually playing duets in that the audio tracks served as the second musician. With "When the Saints Go Marching In" and "Boatman Dance," this is your chance to find someone you know who also plays violin, and practice playing with another live musician. You will play the violin 1 part, and your friend, violin 2. Pay close attention to listening to each other. Both duets are also on the audio, so at first, you may both play along. When comfortable, try playing it together without the audio. Please note that the C♯ on the G string is included in the violin 2 part, a note not introduced in this book.

When the Saints Go Marching In (Duet)

Track 83
Both Violin
Parts

Track 84
Violin 2,
only

Traditional

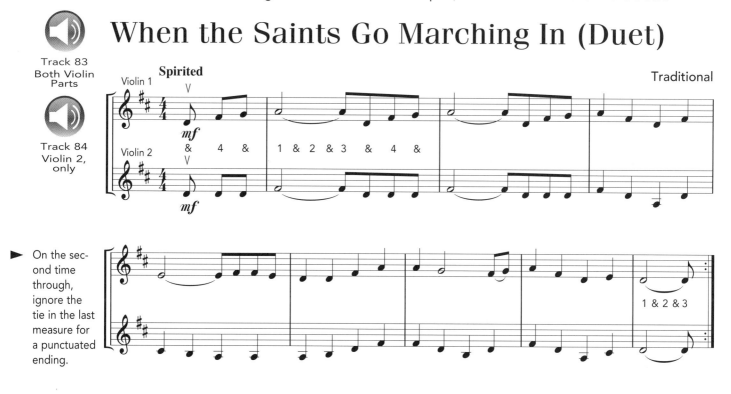

▶ On the second time through, ignore the tie in the last measure for a punctuated ending.

Boatman Dance (Duet)

Track 85
Both Violin
Parts

Track 86
Violin 2,
only

American Folk Song

A Quick Review

Holding Your Violin

With the left hand, pick up your violin by the neck with the strings facing away from you. Hold the instrument where the neck meets the body. If you grab it too close to the pegs, you may "bump" them, throwing the instrument out of tune.

Turn the violin toward you, with the strings facing the ceiling. Bring the violin to your left shoulder placing the side of your left jaw against the chin rest, creating a slight angle between your face and the violin, with the violin angling to the left.

Although it is called a chin rest, your chin never rests directly on the chin rest, rather your jaw is what comes most in contact with it. Slide your left hand toward the pegs, stopping about 1½ inches in front of the nut. Curve your fingers slightly around the neck to touch the strings. Your thumb remains unbent, resting against the left side of the neck. Your left hand cradles the neck in this way, however it does not support the weight of your instrument. Your shoulder and chin support and hold the instrument. Your left wrist should be straight, and your left arm and elbow should be directly beneath the middle of the violin. Practice holding the violin under your chin without your left hand for

several seconds, gradually adding to the amount of time you can support the violin without your left hand. Try to keep your neck and shoulder as relaxed as possible while still supporting the weight of the violin. You may find that a soft sponge or shoulder rest attached beneath the violin will help cushion the space between the violin and your shoulder. This can help make holding the violin more comfortable.

The Bow

Preparing Your Bow

When a bow is stored in its case, the hair is loosened. After taking the bow from your case to play, you will need to tighten the hair by turning the screw clockwise, until the hair is straight and firm, still leaving the stick visibly bowed. Take care not to over tighten the hair, which could damage the bow and produce a harsh sound.

Before playing, rosin the bow by holding the rosin in your left hand while sliding the bow back and forth across the rosin, moving the bow and holding the rosin steady. You will need to apply a little rosin each time you take your violin out to play.

Remember to loosen the bow hair by turning the screw counterclockwise before putting the bow back in the case again.

Holding the Bow

As you learn to hold the bow for the first time, put down your violin so your left hand can assist you. As you become more comfortable with your bow, you will be able to pick it up easily with your right hand alone.

Using your left hand, pick up the bow in the middle of the stick with the hair facing the floor. You should always avoid touching the hair. Place the tip of your right thumb against the spot where the left end of the frog meets the stick, bending your thumb joint slightly.

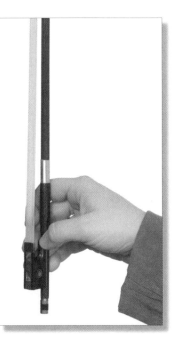

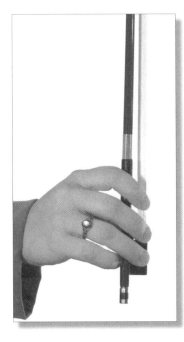

Allow your middle and ring fingers to curve over the stick – your middle finger roughly opposite your thumb, touching the ferrule. The first joint of your index finger will rest along the top of the stick in the middle of the winding, and the tip of your little finger will rest on top of the stick near the screw. Your hand should be relaxed with the fingers spread comfortably. You will want to practice finding this position several times each day until it becomes easy.

The hair should still be facing the floor. Carefully let go of the stick with your left hand. You will notice the weighty feeling on the frog side of the bow.

Learning to properly hold the bow takes a little patience and practice. As you begin to learn notes on the violin, you may wish to pluck the string first, instead of using the bow right away. Plucking a stringed instrument is called "pizzicato." As you play new notes and pieces pizzicato, continue to practice holding the bow to become more comfortable with it.

Tuning Your Violin

The four strings on the violin are tuned to the following pitches, from bottom (low) to top (high): G, D, A, E.

You can adjust each pitch by tightening or loosening each string by turning its corresponding peg. You can make very small adjustments to the string by turning the fine tuners. To tune your violin it is easiest to use an electronic tuner or a piano or keyboard. You may also use a pitch pipe or tuning fork. Track 6 will also enable you to tune your violin. Always tune your instrument before playing.

Violin Care Tip

When placing the violin back in its case, always wipe the rosin off the strings with a soft cloth. This will ensure a longer string life. Also, to protect the wood of the instrument, it is good to place a humidifier in the case during the colder months of the year. Ask for a violin humidifier at your local music store.

Tuning the A String:

Place your violin in playing position with your bow. Listen to the A on the recording, electric tuner, or piano. Play the A on your violin to determine if it matches the A being played. Raise the pitch by turning the corresponding peg slowly and carefully *away* from you. Lower the pitch by turning the peg slowly and carefully *toward* you. If the pitch is very close, use the fine tuner to a make a smaller adjustment. (Not all violins come equipped with fine tuners on all four strings. As a beginner, it is recommended you have a fine tuner on each string.) Turning the fine tuner clockwise **raises** the pitch, counterclockwise **lowers** the pitch. Continue tuning the other three strings in the same manner. The tuning notes are played in the order: A–D–G–E.

Some Tuning Tips:

While tightening or loosening a string, turn the peg or fine tuner slowly, concentrating on the changes in pitch. You might need to pluck the string repeatedly to compare the sound of your string to the note you are tuning to.

As you're tuning a string, you may notice a series of pulsating beat waves. These beat waves can help you tune; they'll slow down as the pitches get closer together, stopping completely when the two pitches are the same, meaning they are in tune.

Instead of tuning a string down to a pitch, tune it up. This allows you to stretch the string into place, which will help it stay in tune longer. If a string is too high in pitch, tune it down first, then bring it back up to pitch. Always be careful not to tune a string too high or too quickly. Strings can break easily as a result, especially the E string.

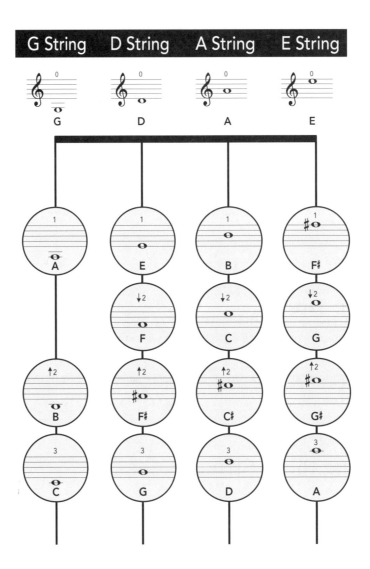

Lesson 11 | Note Review and New Rhythm

The following chart will help you review the notes you've learned so far.

For each musical example, note the key signature and the time signature. Tap the rhythm of each example, and then play *pizzicato* (plucking) the first time, and *arco* (with the bow) the second time.

Easy on the D String

Track 92

Major or Minor?

Track 93

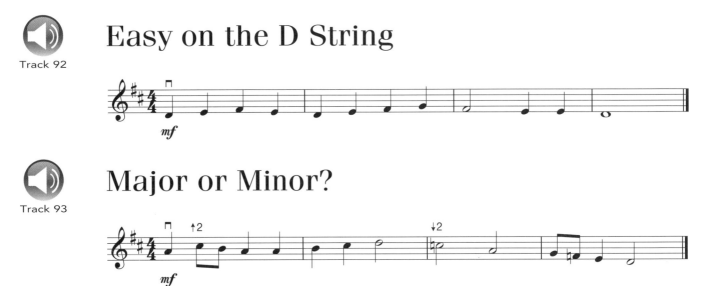

40

Quick Warm-up

Track 94

G String Waltz

Track 95

"Sandy Land" is a well-known American folk tune. Note the key signature, and play *pizzicato*.
All the notes for "Sandy Land" are played on only two strings. Which two strings will you play?

Sandy Land

Track 96

American

Moderately

Place your bow on the D string about two inches from the frog in order to play a short up bow
as you begin "I Gave My Love a Cherry," with a quarter note pick-up. Use smooth, legato bow
strokes for a flowing feel, keeping the bow moving through the half and dotted half notes.

I Gave My Love a Cherry

Track 97

American

Slowly

New Rhythm: Dotted Quarter Note

A dot following a note adds half the note's value.

This rhythm: could also be notated using

a dot as:

In $\frac{4}{4}$ time, a dotted quarter note gets one and a half beats.

Single eighth notes are flagged instead of beamed: ♪ ← flag

Track 98

Practice tapping and counting the rhythm in "Open String Dots." When you are comfortable with the rhythm, try playing this song, first without listening to the recording. Then, listen to Track 99 to see if you played the rhythm correctly, and finally play along with the track.

Track 99

Open String Dots

▶ Write in the counting for the remainder of this song using measures 1–4 as an example.

Look for the dotted rhythms in the Jamaican tune, "Water Come a Me Eye." Tap or clap the first measure. Compare lines one and two: Are they exactly the same? Now compare lines three and four. The form of this piece is "AB." Knowing the form will help you learn the piece more easily.

Track 100

Water Come A Me Eye

▶ Note the slurs under each group of eighth notes and remember that the slur indicates that both notes will be played in one bow stroke, in this case, a down bow.

42

Test Yourself!

Divide the following rhythms into measures by drawing bar lines using the time signatures given. Then, tap and count the rhythms. You may also experiment by playing these rhythms on your violin. Use just one note or attempt to make up your own melody!

Staccato and Dynamics

Before tackling the new tunes in this lesson, warm up slowly with the following exercises using eighth notes. Listen for smooth and even eighths, and in variations one and two, pay close attention to the slurred bowing. To slur two eighth notes, divide your bow stroke into two equal parts. To slur four eighth notes, divide the bow into four parts.

Track 101

Eight to the Bar

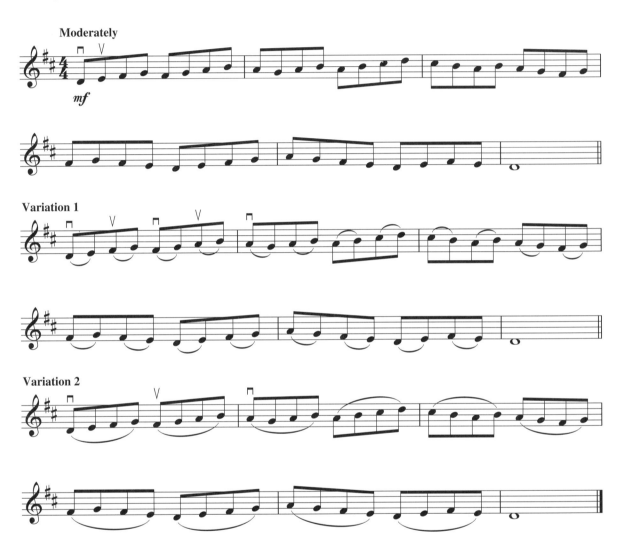

Track 102

Staccato

Staccato notes are written with a dot directly above or below the note head. This indicates a short or detached sound. To create this sound on the violin, a staccato note is played with a stopped bow stroke, creating a small space of silence between the notes.

Stopping for Staccato

Track 103

Staccato notes give "Theme from Symphony No. 94" a light-hearted and humorous feel. Use just a small amount of bow for each stopped bow stroke when playing *staccato*.

Theme from Symphony No. 94

Track 104

► Remember to lift your bow where indicated in order to prepare for another down bow on the next note.

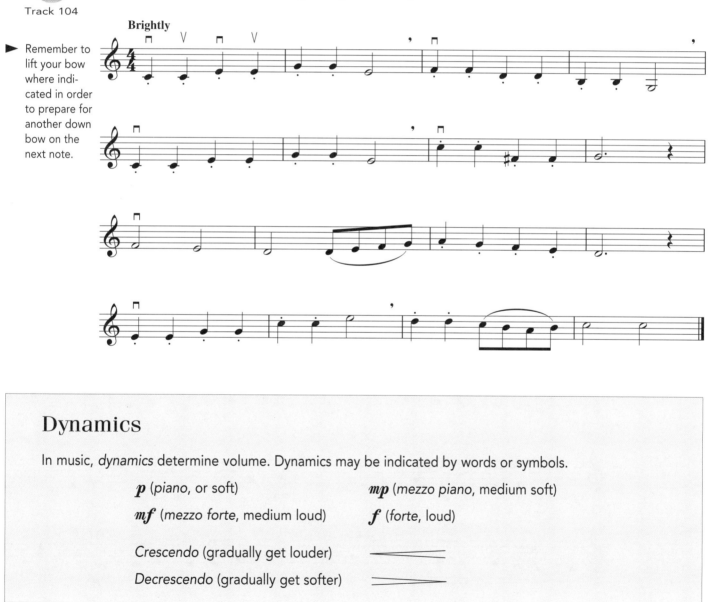

Dynamics

In music, *dynamics* determine volume. Dynamics may be indicated by words or symbols.

p (piano, or soft)   *mp* (mezzo piano, medium soft)

mf (mezzo forte, medium loud)   *f* (forte, loud)

Crescendo (gradually get louder)

Decrescendo (gradually get softer)

45

Before playing "Father Put the Cow Out," look through the piece and note the many dynamic changes. Play with more weight in the bow for a louder sound, and less weight for a softer sound.

Track 105

Father Put the Cow Out

American

► Notice how measures 9–10 are *staccato*, but 11–12 are not. Work on making a difference in the style between these two groups of measures.

Track 106

"Long, Long Ago" is a well-known tune with a beautiful flowing melody. Practice the crescendo and decrescendo until you achieve the sound you desire. Keep the bow moving through the notes to produce a singing legato tone. In the last measure, the fermata sign indicates that you may hold the last note as long as you wish.

Track 107

Long, Long Ago

T. H. Bayly

46

A New Scale

Playing the G Major Scale

A major scale consists of eight notes in the following pattern of whole and half steps:

Starting note–W–W–H–W–W–W–H

Beginning on G, following this pattern of half and whole steps gives us the notes
G–A–B–C–D–E–F♯–G.

Playing major scales are a great warm-up, and are beneficial to understanding fingering patterns.

Play the following two-octave G major scale with detached bowing, changing the bow stroke
on every note. You may also play the scale *pizzicato*. Listen carefully for accurate intonation.

G Major Scale

Chords and Arpeggios

A *chord* consists of three or more notes played at the same time or *harmonically*. The notes of
a chord are often the interval of a third apart, as in the following G chord:

Chords are most often played on instruments such as piano or guitar.

An *arpeggio* (sometimes referred to as a "broken chord") is a chord with the notes played one
at a time or *melodically*. A G major chord would consist of the first, third, and fifth notes of the
G major scale.

Playing *arpeggios* is an excellent way to work on accurate intonation. Play the following *arpeggio* using the notes from the G major scale.

G Arpeggio

Notice the musical signs above measures 4–5, and 6–7 in the next piece, "St. Anthony Chorale." These are called *first* and *second endings.* After playing measures 4–5 (first ending) follow the repeat sign back to the beginning, but this time, after playing measure 3, skip to the second ending to play measures 6–7.

St. Anthony Chorale

F. J. Haydn

Hooked Bowing

Hooked bowing is when two (or more) notes are played in the same direction with a stop in the motion of the bow between the notes, notated like this:

Practice hooked bowing as you play "By Hook or by Crook." The quarter notes will have short, stopped bow strokes.

By Hook or By Crook

Track 116

"Theme from Symphony No. 9" uses a dotted rhythm throughout. Clap and count this rhythm, then play the notes *pizzicato* to become familiar with this famous tune. When you're ready to use the bow, notice that a hooked bowing is used to connect the dotted quarter and eighth notes. Remember to use a longer stroke for the dotted quarter, and a short stroke for the eighth note.

Theme from Symphony No. 9

Track 117

Dvorak

Track 118

Johann Sebastian Bach (1685–1750) is a well-known composer from the Baroque period. He wrote many works for string instruments, as well as for woodwind, voice, and keyboard. "Minuet" is a slow and graceful dance in $\frac{3}{4}$ time. Use a hooked bowing in the first measure as indicated. Listen to the dance-like rhythmic feel which should result from playing the repeated notes bowed in this way.

Minuet

Track 119

J.S. Bach

New Note on the D String

Track 120

New Note: A on the D String

Placing the fourth finger on a string matches the pitch of the next highest open string. For example, finger 4 on the D string is the same pitch as the open A string.

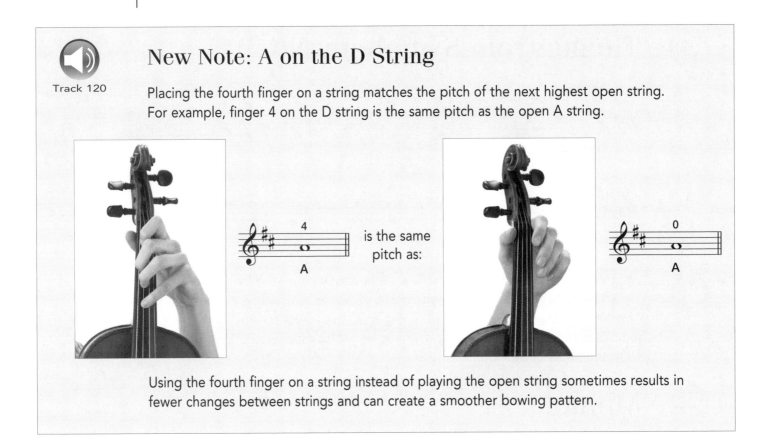

Using the fourth finger on a string instead of playing the open string sometimes results in fewer changes between strings and can create a smoother bowing pattern.

By using finger 4 on the D string, "Ode to Joy" can be played entirely on one string.

Track 121

Ode to Joy

"German Folk Song" can also be played entirely on the D string.

German Folk Song

German

Play the D major scale below. Notice that A is played as an open string going up the scale (ascending), but is played with finger 4 on the D string going down the scale (descending).

D Major Scale

Try the same fingering when playing the D major *arpeggio*. Play open A when ascending, then finger 4 on the D string when descending.

D Major Arpeggio

"French Folk Song" is a lovely flowing tune. Use plenty of bow on the repeated notes for a smooth *legato* sound, and pay special care to the dynamics marked.

Track 125

French Folk Song

French

▶ Experiment by adding your own bowings such as hooked bowings on repeated notes and additional slurs. Pencil in your new bowings and use them to help play the song more expressively.

Test Yourself!

Name the string and finger number you would use to play the notes given. Example one is done for you.

New Note on the G String

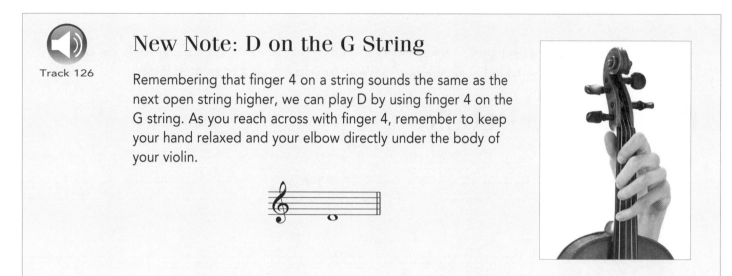

Track 126

New Note: D on the G String

Remembering that finger 4 on a string sounds the same as the next open string higher, we can play D by using finger 4 on the G string. As you reach across with finger 4, remember to keep your hand relaxed and your elbow directly under the body of your violin.

As you play "Delightfully D" listen for the G-string D and the open-string D to sound the same.

Track 127

Delightfully D

Moderately

Track 128

The key of C major has no sharps or flats in the key signature. Play the following scales and *arpeggios* with precise eighth-note rhythms. Play at a slow tempo first, and then challenge yourself by increasing the tempo while keeping the eighth notes steady. You may wish to use a metronome to assist you.

Track 129

C Major Scale

► In addition to playing the dynamics as written, try the opposite: begin *forte* and *decrescendo* during the first line, then *crescendo* on the second line, ending *forte*.

C Major Arpeggio

Track 130

Watch for slurs as you play "Yankee Doodle." Notice that all of the Ds are played on the open string except for the last D in measure 15. Work toward a lively and spirited tempo.

Yankee Doodle

Track 131

American

Track 132

In the Russian folk song "Come Beautiful May," be sure to lift your bow at the rest in measure 2, and play measure 3 softly, like an echo. The D in the next to the last measure will be played with finger 4 on the G string.

Come Beautiful May

Track 133

Russian folk song

Test Yourself!

Can you complete the following tunes? Use your ears and fingers to guide you as you hum or sing along. Attempt to play the missing notes on your violin, and when you think you have it, write the notes in the empty measures.

Alouette

London Bridge

Oh, Susanna

A Major Scale and Arpeggio

The key of A major has three sharps: F#, C#, and G#. The following scale exercise asks you to slur two notes to a bow and then four notes to a bow. Be patient as you practice dividing the bow equally between the notes.

Track 134

A Major Scale

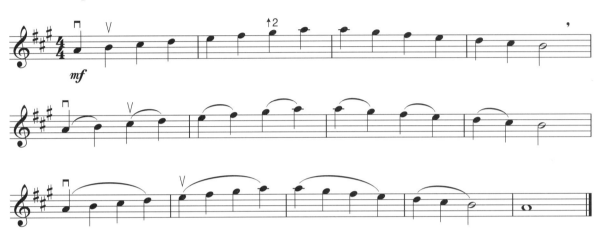

Slurring *arpeggios* is a bit trickier, but you can do it! Play slowly, concentrating on good intonation, string crossing, and the speed of your bow.

Track 135

Arpeggios to Slur

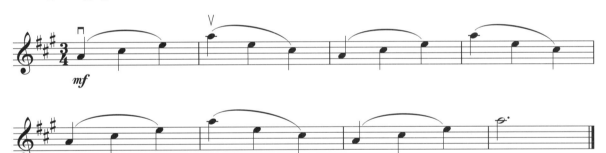

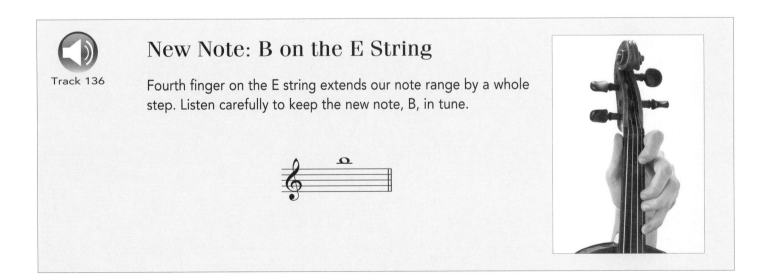

Track 136

New Note: B on the E String

Fourth finger on the E string extends our note range by a whole step. Listen carefully to keep the new note, B, in tune.

Track 137

Easy Does It

The American folk song "Sourwood Mountain" is a traditional old-time dance tune dating back to the early 1900s, originating in the southern mountain region. Try to capture some dance-like energy as you play this tune handed down from generation to generation.

Track 138

Sourwood Mountain

American

► Notice that the dynamics change when you take the repeats. Try to make a noticeable dynamic contrast.

"Arkansas Traveler" is another traditional fiddle tune. First play it *pizzicato* to familiarize yourself with the melody. When playing it *arco*, play the tune slowly at first, paying close attention to the bowing marked. Then, increase to a lively dance tempo.

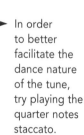
Track 139

Arkansas Traveler

American

► In order to better facilitate the dance nature of the tune, try playing the quarter notes staccato.

Also known as "Simple Gifts," "Shaker Melody" originated in the mid 1800s as a dance tune. It became widely known after the composer Aaron Copland (1900-1990) used the melody in his famous orchestral work *Appalachian Spring*. More recently, this tune was featured in "Air and Simple Gifts" by John Williams (b. 1932), and was played at the inauguration of U.S. President Barack Obama. Play this tune with a moderate tempo and smooth bow strokes.

Shaker Melody

Traditional Shaker hymn

Lesson 17 | New G and A String Notes

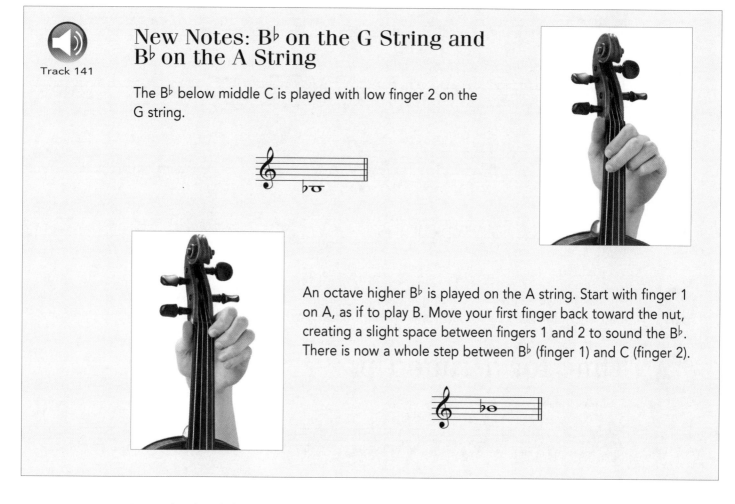

Track 141

New Notes: B♭ on the G String and B♭ on the A String

The B♭ below middle C is played with low finger 2 on the G string.

An octave higher B♭ is played on the A string. Start with finger 1 on A, as if to play B. Move your first finger back toward the nut, creating a slight space between fingers 1 and 2 to sound the B♭. There is now a whole step between B♭ (finger 1) and C (finger 2).

Listen for the darker, minor sound in "Unhappy Camper" which uses the low B♭ on the G string.

Track 142

Unhappy Camper

59

Listen for the whole step in "Interval Waltz" which makes use of the higher B♭, on the G string.

Track 143

Interval Waltz

Track 144

All string players strive for accurate intonation. A great way to practice this is to work on matching intervals. "Time for a Tune-Up" includes major, minor, and perfect intervals.

Track 145

Time for a Tune-Up

▶ Listen carefully to the half-step difference between intervals such as D–F compared to D–F♯.

Note the bowing pattern at the beginning of "Kum Ba Yah." Keep the bow moving slowly and steadily as you play. This will produce a smooth, legato sound, and give you plenty of bow for the whole notes.

Track 146

Kum Ba Yah

African

Track 147

Plan ahead for the G♯ in measure 2 of "Brightness of My Day." You may wish to play this tune *pizzicato* first to practice the difference between G and G♯. Count carefully, and look out for the ties across the bar line.

Track 148

Brightness of My Day

Another tune with long bows is "Down in the Valley." As this is a slow waltz, you will need a long, slow bow to play the tied dotted half notes. Use the rests to breathe and lift the bow, starting each new phrase with a down bow.

Track 149

Down in the Valley

American

Test Yourself!

Name the following intervals in the key of G major. Sing the intervals, and then play them.

2nd

New Note on the E String

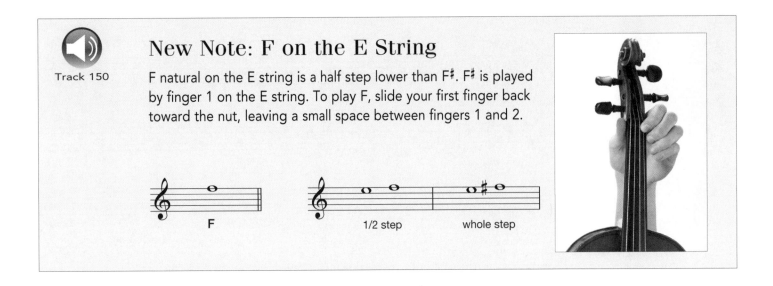

New Note: F on the E String

F natural on the E string is a half step lower than F♯. F♯ is played by finger 1 on the E string. To play F, slide your first finger back toward the nut, leaving a small space between fingers 1 and 2.

Track 150

F

1/2 step   whole step

Play "Whole or Half?" to hear the difference between F natural and F♯.

Whole or Half?

Track 151

► Accidentals do not carry over the bar line. However, as a reminder, a cautionary accidental may be included as in measure 4.

The F major scale includes our new note F, and also B♭ from Lesson 17. Note the B♭ in the F major key signature. This exercise uses quarter notes, then doubles the rhythm to eighth notes.

F Major Scale

Track 152

Continue to work on slurred bowing while practicing "F Major Arpeggio." Play slowly, and with excellent intonation.

Track 153

► Experiment by playing this with alternate bowings such as one bow per quarter note or two-then-one-bow for quarter notes.

F Major Arpeggio

Play the notes of "Lament" *pizzicato* until you become comfortable playing F natural. This tune should be played slowly, with long full bow strokes to portray its mournful character.

Track 154

Lament

Track 155

$\frac{6}{8}$ Time Signature

One may think of $\frac{6}{8}$ time as having six beats to a measure, with an eighth note receiving one beat.

$\frac{6}{8}$ 6 beats per measure
♪ = 1 beat

Another way to count $\frac{6}{8}$ time is as two beats per measure, in other words, the dotted quarter note gets one beat.

$\frac{6}{8}$ or $\frac{2}{♩.}$

Tap the rhythms in the examples below before playing them on the open strings.
Count six beats per measure for slower tempos.

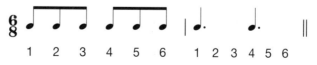

But you may wish to count two beats per measure for faster tempos.

Slow and Steady

Track 156

Quick as a Wink

Track 157

Count two beats per measure when you play "Oh, Dear, What Can the Matter Be?" Practice slurring three notes to a bow as marked.

Oh, Dear, What Can the Matter Be?

Track 158

American

► When first learning a tune, you may start slowly, counting six beats to a measure, then change to two beats per measure as you play the tune faster.

"Irish Folk Song" is a slow tune with a touch of melancholy. Count six beats to each measure and play with a smooth legato bow.

Irish Folk Song

Track 159

Irish

Sixteenth Notes

Sixteenth Notes

Sixteenth notes are played twice as fast as eighth notes. Four sixteenth notes equal one quarter note. Sixteenth notes can be flagged or beamed. (Note: sixteenth notes will almost always be beamed together when in a group of two or four that start on the beat. Flags are used in more complex rhythms involving single sixteenth notes.)

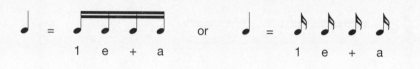

Clap and count the following sixteenth note rhythms in each song before playing them on your violin.

Sweet Sixteen

Track 161

Pretty Little Girl with the Red Dress On

Track 162

American

Moderately

1 e + a 2 (e) + a   1 (e + a) 2 (e + a)

mp

mf

f

Skip to My Lou

Track 163

American

Moderately

▶ Pay careful
attention to
the rhythms in
measures 9,
11, and 13.

1 + 2 + 1 + a 2 +

mf

p   *mp*

mf   *f*

"Cumberland Mountain Bear Chase" is an American folk song in the fiddle tradition. Tap the rhythm before playing and keep your bow strokes short on the sixteenth notes to give this tune plenty of dance-like energy.

Track 164

Cumberland Mountain Bear Chase

► In measure 12, lift your bow quickly after the quarter note.

A well-known tune from the Gold Rush era, the American folk song "Sweet Betsy from Pike" is played on the lower strings. Use lots of energy, and pay close attention to the dynamic markings throughout. Familiarize yourself with the key signature, time signature, and fingering. Play the tune *pizzicato* the first time through and *arco* the second.

Track 165

Sweet Betsy

Test Yourself!

Divide the following rhythms into measures according to the time signature given. Include a final double bar line at the end. Remember that the bottom number of the time signature determines which note receives one beat.

Once you've added bar lines, clap and count the rhythms and then play each example on your violin. You may first play the rhythms on one pitch of your choice. Then, improvise your own melody notes while playing the rhythms. Have fun and experiment!

Lesson 20 | The Basics

Track 166

Shifting

Shifting on a string instrument is moving your hand to different places on the fingerboard. Up until now your hand has stayed close to the scroll in what is called *first position*. Shifting allows you to extend the range of notes you can play on any one string, and also makes it easier to move between notes and strings. There are seven positions on the violin, but the most commonly used positions for intermediate violinists are first position and third position.

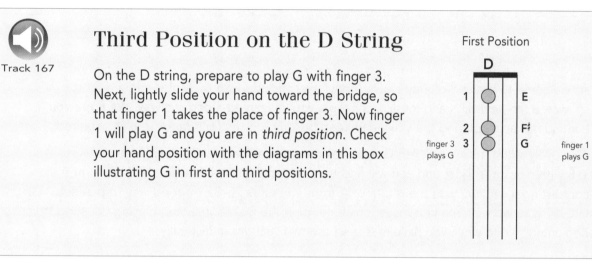

Track 167

Third Position on the D String

On the D string, prepare to play G with finger 3. Next, lightly slide your hand toward the bridge, so that finger 1 takes the place of finger 3. Now finger 1 will play G and you are in *third position*. Check your hand position with the diagrams in this box illustrating G in first and third positions.

Moving finger 1 to third position allows you to play higher notes on the D string. Shifts/positions are marked with Roman numerals. Try shifting to third position in "Ready, Set, Shift!"

Ready, Set, Shift!

Track 168

► Listen carefully to make sure the two Gs in measures 2 and 3 are in tune with each other.

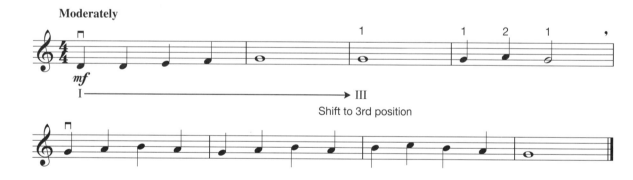

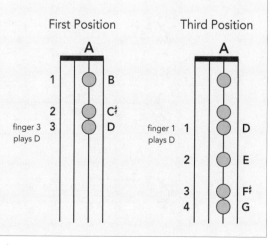

Track 169

Third Position on the A String

Shifting to third position is the same for each string: finger 1 takes the place of finger 3. On the A string, play D with finger 3. Now shift finger 1 toward the bridge to play D. You've found third position!

69

"Night Shift" starts in first position on the A string, shifts to third position, and then shifts back to first position.

Night Shift

As we come to the end of *Play Violin Today!* we conclude with two solos and a duet to showcase the new skills and musical concepts you've learned along the way. We hope you continue to enjoy playing the violin and keep building on the foundation you've acquired!

The lovely Welsh folk song "Ash Grove" has the musical form AABA. Compare measures 1–8 with measures 9–16, and you will find they are exactly alike. Measures 17–24 form the contrasting B section, with the return of A from measures 25–32. A good way to practice "Ash Grove" is to work on the first A section alone, then the B section alone, playing the song from beginning to end when you have mastered the two sections individually.

Ash Grove

American

70

"Minuet" is from *French Suite VI* by J.S. Bach. A classic dance from the Baroque period, the minuet is characterized by its **¾** meter and graceful style. Note the hooked bowing as marked.

Track 172

Minuet

J.S. Bach

Track 173

Our final tune, "Shenandoah," is arranged for two violins. Part One plays the melody throughout. You could play this part as a solo. To play the duet, find a friend or teacher to play the second violin part with you, or play along with the recording (Track 174 features a demo of both violin parts while Track 175 only plays the violin two part). Learn the second violin part as well, so you can switch parts with your partner, or play along with the recording.

Track 174
Demo

Track 175
Play-Along

Shenandoah

American

Fingering Charts

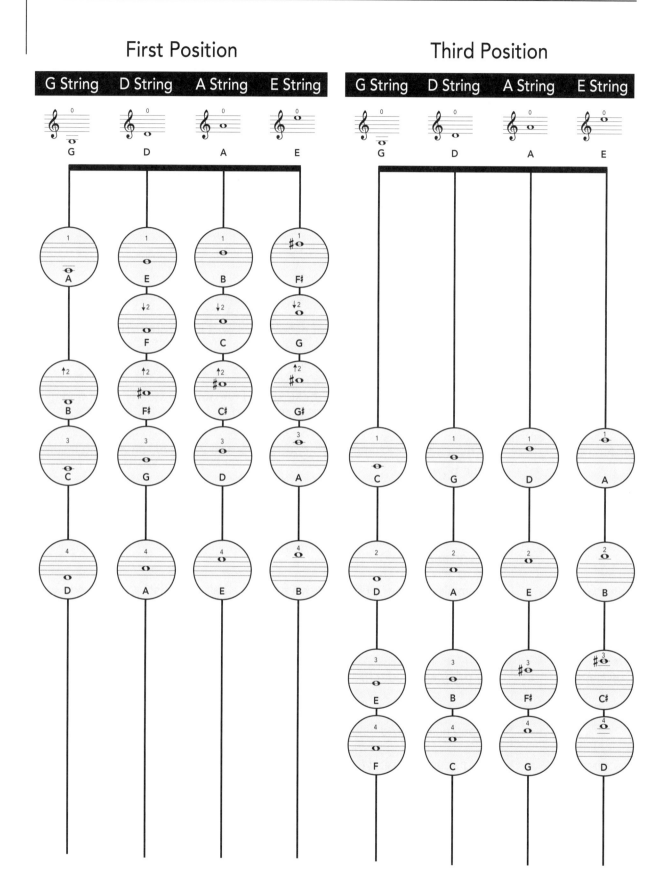

First Position

G String	D String	A String	E String

Third Position

G String	D String	A String	E String

Glossary of Musical Terms

1st and 2nd ending	The 1st and 2nd ending signs are similar to the repeat sign. Play through the music until the repeat sign, playing the first ending. Then when repeating the music, go directly to the 2nd ending, skipping the music marked as "1st ending."
Accent	An Accent mark (>) means to emphasize the note to which it is attached.
Accidental	Any sharp (♯), flat (♭), or natural (♮) sign that appears in the music but is not in the key signature.
Allegro	Fast tempo.
Andante	Slower "walking" tempo.
Arco	With the bow.
Arpeggio	The notes of a chord played in succession, one note at a time.
Bass Clef (𝄢)	(F Clef) indicates the position of note names on a music staff. The fourth line in bass clef is F.
Bar Lines	Bar Lines divide the music staff into measures.
Beat	The pulse of music, like a heartbeat, should remain very steady. Counting aloud and foot-tapping help maintain a steady beat.
Breath Mark	The Breath Mark (❜) indicates a specific place to inhale or, on a string instrument, a place to lift the bow.
Chord	When two or more notes are played together, they form a chord or harmony.
Chromatic Notes	Chromatic Notes are altered with sharps, flats and natural signs which are not in the key signature.
Chromatic Scale	The smallest distance between two notes is a half step, and a scale made up of consecutive half steps is called a Chromatic Scale.
Common Time	Common Time (𝄴) is the same as $\frac{4}{4}$ time signature.
Crescendo	Play gradually louder. (*cresc.*)
D.C. al Fine	Play again from the beginning, stopping at Fine. D.C. is the abbreviation for Da Capo, or "to the beginning," and Fine means "the end."
Decrescendo	Play gradually softer. (*decresc.*)
Diminuendo	Same as decrescendo. (*dim.*)
Dotted Half Note	A note three beats long in duration. (𝅗𝅥.) A dot adds half the value of the original note.
Double Bar (𝄁)	Indicates the end of a piece of music.
Down Bow (⊓)	Drawing the bow downward, towards the floor.
Duet	A composition with two different parts played together.
Dynamics	Dynamics indicate how loud or soft to play a passage of music.

Eighth Note	An Eighth Note (♪) receives half the value of a quarter note, that is, half a beat. Two or more eighth notes are usually joined together with a beam, as follows: ♫
Eighth Rest	Indicates ½ beat of silence. (𝄾)
Enharmonics	Two notes that are written differently, but sound the same (and played with the same fingering) are called Enharmonics (F♯ and G♭).
Fermata	The Fermata (𝄐) indicates that a note (or rest) is held somewhat longer than normal.
Flat (♭)	Lowers the note a half step and remains in effect for the entire measure.
Forte (𝆑)	Play loudly.
Half Note	A Half Note (𝅗𝅥) receives two beats. It's equal in length to two quarter notes.
Half Rest	The Half Rest (▬) marks two beats of silence.
Half Step	The smallest interval in Western music; on the piano, from one key to the very next key.
Harmony	Two or more notes played together.
Hooked Bowing	Two or more notes bowed in the same direction, with a stop in between the notes.
Interval	The distance between two pitches.
Key Signature	A Key Signature (the group of sharps or flats before the time signature) tells which notes are played as sharps or flats throughout the entire piece.
Largo	A very slow tempo.
Ledger Lines	Ledger Lines extend the music staff. Notes on ledger lines can be above or below the staff.
Legato	Play in a smooth manner, slurred.
Major Scale	Eight notes in succession, with half steps between the third and fourth, and seventh and eighth degrees, whole steps between all the others.
Mezzo Forte (𝐦𝆑)	Moderately loud.
Mezzo Piano (𝐦𝐩)	Moderately soft.
Minuet	A dance of French origin from the 1600s in 3/4 time.
Moderato	Medium or moderate tempo.
Music Staff	The Music Staff has 5 lines and 4 spaces where notes and rests are written.
Natural Sign (♮)	Cancels a flat ♭ or sharp ♯ and remains in effect for the entire measure.
Notes	Notes tell us how high or low to play by their placement on a line or space of the music staff, and how long to play.
Phrase	A Phrase is a musical "sentence," often 2 or 4 measures long.

Piano (p)	Soft.
Pitch	The highness or lowness of a note which is indicated by the horizontal placement of the note on the music staff.
Pick-Up Notes	One or more notes that come before the first full measure. The beats of Pick-Up Notes are subtracted from the last measure—also called "upbeats."
Pizzicato	Plucked.
Quarter Note	A Quarter Note (♩) receives one beat. There are 4 quarter notes in a $\frac{4}{4}$ measure.
Quarter Rest	The Quarter Rest (𝄽) marks one beat of silence.
Repeat Sign	The Repeat Sign (:‖) means to play once again from the beginning without pause. Repeat the section of music enclosed by the repeat signs (‖▭‖). If 1st and 2nd endings are used, they are played as usual—but go back only to the first repeat sign, not to the beginning.
Rests	Beats of silence.
Rhythm	Rhythm refers to time—how long, or for how many beats a note lasts, including rests.
Scale	A sequence of notes in ascending or descending order. Like a musical "ladder," each step is the next consecutive note in the musical alphabet.
Sharp (♯)	Raises the note a half step and remains in effect for the entire measure.
Shifting	On a string instrument, moving the left hand to different places on the fingerboard.
Slur	A curved line connecting notes of different pitch.
Staccato	Play in a short, separated manner.
Stopped Bow	Play in a detached style, with a small space of silence between the notes.
Tempo	The speed of music.
Tie	A curved line connecting two notes of the same pitch. A tie between two notes makes the first note last the value of both notes "tied" together.
Time Signature	Indicates how many beats per measure and what kind of note gets one beat.
Treble Clef (𝄞)	(G Clef) indicates the position of note names on a music staff: The second line in Treble Clef is G.
Up Bow (∨)	Drawing the bow upward, towards you.
Upbeat	See "pick-up note."
Whole Note	A Whole Note (𝅝) lasts for four full beats (a complete measure in $\frac{4}{4}$ time).
Whole Rest	The Whole Rest (𝄻) indicates a whole measure of silence.
Whole Step	Two half steps, also called a "second."

Play Today! Series

The Ultimate Self-Teaching Series

These are complete guides to the basics, designed to offer quality instruction, terrific songs, and professional-quality audio with tons of full-demo tracks and instruction. Each book includes over 70 great songs and examples!

Play Accordion Today!
00701744	Level 1 Book/Audio	$10.99
00702657	Level 1 Songbook Book/Audio	$12.99

Play Alto Sax Today!
00842049	Level 1 Book/Audio	$9.99
00842050	Level 2 Book/Audio	$9.99
00320359	DVD	$14.95
00842051	Songbook Book/Audio	$12.95
00699555	Beginner's – Level 1 Book/Audio & DVD	$19.95
00699492	Play Today Plus Book/Audio	$14.95

Play Banjo Today!
00699897	Level 1 Book/Audio	$9.99
00701006	Level 2 Book/Audio	$9.99
00320913	DVD	$14.99
00115999	Songbook Book/Audio	$12.99
00701873	Beginner's – Level 1 Book/Audio & DVD	$19.95

Play Bass Today!
00842020	Level 1 Book/Audio	$9.99
00842036	Level 2 Book/Audio	$9.99
00320356	DVD	$14.95
00842037	Songbook Book/Audio	$12.95
00699552	Beginner's – Level 1 Book/Audio & DVD	$19.99

Play Cello Today!
00151353	Level 1 Book/Audio	$9.99

Play Clarinet Today!
00842046	Level 1 Book/Audio	$9.99
00842047	Level 2 Book/Audio	$9.99
00320358	DVD	$14.95
00842048	Songbook Book/Audio	$12.95
00699554	Beginner's – Level 1 Book/Audio & DVD	$19.95
00699490	Play Today Plus Book/Audio	$14.95

Play Dobro Today!
00701505	Level 1 Book/Audio	$9.99

Play Drums Today!
00842021	Level 1 Book/Audio	$9.99
00842038	Level 2 Book/Audio	$9.95
00320355	DVD	$14.95
00842039	Songbook Book/Audio	$12.95
00699551	Beginner's – Level 1 Book/Audio & DVD	$19.95
00703291	Starter	$24.99

Play Flute Today
00842043	Level 1 Book/Audio	$9.95
00842044	Level 2 Book/Audio	$9.99
00320360	DVD	$14.95
00842045	Songbook Book/Audio	$12.95
00699553	Beginner's – Level 1 Book/Audio & DVD	$19.95

Play Guitar Today!
00696100	Level 1 Book/Audio	$9.99
00696101	Level 2 Book/Audio	$9.99
00320353	DVD	$14.95
00696102	Songbook Book/Audio	$12.99
00699544	Beginner's – Level 1 Book/Audio & DVD	$19.95
00702431	Worship Songbook Book/Audio	$12.99
00695662	Complete Kit	$29.95

Play Harmonica Today!
00700179	Level 1 Book/Audio	$9.99
00320653	DVD	$14.99
00701875	Beginner's – Level 1 Book/Audio & DVD	$19.95

Play Mandolin Today!
00699911	Level 1 Book/Audio	$9.99
00320909	DVD	$14.99
00115029	Songbook Book/Audio	$12.99
00701874	Beginner's – Level 1 Book/Audio & DVD	$19.99

Play Piano Today!
Revised Edition
00842019	Level 1 Book/Audio	$9.99
00298773	Level 2 Book/Audio	$9.95
00842041	Songbook Book/Audio	$12.95
00699545	Beginner's – Level 1 Book/Audio & DVD	$19.95
00702415	Worship Songbook Book/Audio	$12.99
00703707	Complete Kit	$22.99

Play Recorder Today!
00700919	Level 1 Book/Audio	$7.99
00119830	Complete Kit	$19.99

Sing Today!
00699761	Level 1 Book/Audio	$10.99

Play Trombone Today!
00699917	Level 1 Book/Audio	$12.99
00320508	DVD	$14.95

Play Trumpet Today!
00842052	Level 1 Book/Audio	$9.99
00842053	Level 2 Book/Audio	$9.95
00320357	DVD	$14.95
00842054	Songbook Book/Audio	$12.95
00699556	Beginner's – Level 1 Book/Audio & DVD	$19.95

Play Ukulele Today!
00699638	Level 1 Book/Audio	$10.99
00699655	Play Today Plus Book/Audio	$9.99
00320985	DVD	$14.99
00701872	Beginner's – Level 1 Book/Audio & DVD	$19.95
00650743	Book/Audio/DVD with Ukulele	$39.99
00701002	Level 2 Book/Audio	$9.99
00702484	Level 2 Songbook Book/Audio	$12.99
00703290	Starter	$24.99

Play Viola Today!
00142679	Level 1 Book/Audio	$9.99

Play Violin Today!
00699748	Level 1 Book/Audio	$9.99
00701320	Level 2 Book/Audio	$9.99
00321076	DVD	$14.99
00701700	Songbook Book/Audio	$12.99
00701876	Beginner's – Level 1 Book/Audio & DVD	$19.95

HAL•LEONARD®
www.halleonard.com

HAL•LEONARD® VIOLIN PLAY-ALONG

AUDIO ACCESS INCLUDED

The Violin Play-Along Series

Play your favorite songs quickly and easily!

Just follow the music, listen to the CD or online audio to hear how the violin should sound, and then play along using the separate backing tracks. The audio files are enhanced so you can adjust the recordings to any tempo without changing pitch!

1. Bluegrass
00842152 ....$14.99

2. Popular Songs
00842153 ....$16.99

3. Classical
00842154 ....$16.99

4. Celtic
00842155 ....$14.99

5. Christmas Carols
00842156 ....$14.99

6. Classic Christmas Songs
00348311 ....$14.99

7. Jazz
00842196 ....$16.99

8. Country Classics
00842230 ....$14.99

9. Country Hits
00842231 ....$14.99

10. Bluegrass Favorites
00842232 ....$14.99

11. Bluegrass Classics
00842233 ....$16.99

12. Wedding Classics
00842324 ....$14.99

13. Wedding Favorites
00842325 ....$16.99

14. Blues Classics
00842427 ....$14.99

15. Stephane Grappelli
00842428 ....$16.99

16. Folk Songs
00842429 ....$14.99

17. Christmas Favorites
00842478 ....$14.99

18. Fiddle Hymns
00842499 ....$14.99

19. Lennon & McCartney
00842564 ....$14.99

20. Irish Tunes
00842565 ....$16.99

21. Andrew Lloyd Webber
00842566 ....$16.99

22. Broadway Hits
00842567 ....$14.99

23. Pirates of the Caribbean
00842625 ....$16.99

24. Rock Classics
00842640 ....$14.99

25. Classical Masterpieces
00842642 ....$14.99

26. Elementary Classics
00842643 ....$14.99

27. Classical Favorites
00842646 ....$14.99

28. Classical Treasures
00842647 ....$14.99

29. Disney Favorites
00842648 ....$16.99

30. Disney Hits
00842649 ....$14.99

31. Movie Themes
00842706 ....$14.99

32. Favorite Christmas Songs
00102110 ....$14.99

33. Hoedown
00102161 ....$14.99

34. Barn Dance
00102568 ....$14.99

35. Lindsey Stirling
00109715 ....$19.99

36. Hot Jazz
00110373 ....$14.99

37. Taylor Swift
00116361 ....$14.99

38. John Williams
00116367 ....$16.99

39. Italian Songs
00116368 ....$14.99

40. Trans-Siberian Orchestra
00119909 ....$19.99

41. Johann Strauss
00121041 ....$14.99

42. Light Classics
00121935 ....$14.99

43. Light Orchestra Pop
00122126 ....$14.99

44. French Songs
00122123 ....$14.99

45. Lindsey Stirling Hits
00123128 ....$19.99

46. Piazzolla Tangos
48022997 ....$16.99

47. Light Masterworks
00124149 ....$14.99

48. Frozen
00126478 ....$14.99

49. Pop/Rock
00130216 ....$14.99

50. Songs for Beginners
00131417 ....$14.99

51. Chart Hits for Beginners – 2nd Ed.
00293887 ....$14.99

52. Celtic Rock
00148756 ....$16.99

53. Rockin' Classics
00148768 ....$14.99

54. Scottish Folksongs
00148779 ....$14.99

55. Wicked
00148780 ....$14.99

56. The Sound of Music
00148782 ....$14.99

57. Movie Music
00150962 ....$14.99

58. The Piano Guys – Wonders
00151837 ....$19.99

59. Worship Favorites
00152534 ....$14.99

60. The Beatles
00155293 ....$16.99

61. Star Wars: The Force Awakens
00157648 ....$14.99

62. Star Wars
00157650 ....$14.99

63. George Gershwin
00159612 ....$14.99

64. Lindsey Stirling Favorites
00159634 ....$19.99

65. Taylor Davis
00190208 ....$19.99

66. Pop Covers
00194642 ....$14.99

67. Love Songs
00211896 ....$14.99

68. Queen
00221964 ....$14.99

69. La La Land
00232247 ....$17.99

70. Metallica
00242929 ....$14.99

71. Andrew Lloyd Webber Hits
00244688 ....$14.99

72. Lindsey Stirling – Selections from Warmer in the Winter
00254923 ....$19.99

73. Taylor Davis Favorites
00256297 ....$19.99

74. The Piano Guys – Christmas Together
00262873 ....$19.99

75. Ed Sheeran
00274194 ....$16.99

76. Cajun & Zydeco Songs
00338131 ....$14.99

77. Favorite Christmas Hymns
00278017 ....$14.99

78. Hillsong Worship Hits
00279512 ....$14.99

79. Lindsey Stirling – Top Songs
00284305 ....$19.99

80. Gypsy Jazz
00293922 ....$14.99

81. Lindsey Stirling – Christmas Collection
00298588 ....$19.99

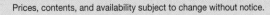

HAL•LEONARD®

www.halleonard.com

HAL·LEONARD INSTRUMENTAL PLAY-ALONG

Your favorite songs are arranged just for solo instrumentalists with this outstanding series. Each book includes great full-accompaniment play-along audio so you can sound just like a pro!

Check out **halleonard.com** for songlists and more titles!

12 Pop Hits
12 songs
00261790	Flute	00261795	Horn
00261791	Clarinet	00261796	Trombone
00261792	Alto Sax	00261797	Violin
00261793	Tenor Sax	00261798	Viola
00261794	Trumpet	00261799	Cello

The Very Best of Bach
15 selections
00225371	Flute	00225376	Horn
00225372	Clarinet	00225377	Trombone
00225373	Alto Sax	00225378	Violin
00225374	Tenor Sax	00225379	Viola
00225375	Trumpet	00225380	Cello

The Beatles
15 songs
00225330	Flute	00225335	Horn
00225331	Clarinet	00225336	Trombone
00225332	Alto Sax	00225337	Violin
00225333	Tenor Sax	00225338	Viola
00225334	Trumpet	00225339	Cello

Chart Hits
12 songs
00146207	Flute	00146212	Horn
00146208	Clarinet	00146213	Trombone
00146209	Alto Sax	00146214	Violin
00146210	Tenor Sax	00146211	Trumpet
00146216	Cello		

Christmas Songs
12 songs
00146855	Flute	00146863	Horn
00146858	Clarinet	00146864	Trombone
00146859	Alto Sax	00146866	Violin
00146860	Tenor Sax	00146867	Viola
00146862	Trumpet	00146868	Cello

Contemporary Broadway
15 songs
00298704	Flute	00298709	Horn
00298705	Clarinet	00298710	Trombone
00298706	Alto Sax	00298711	Violin
00298707	Tenor Sax	00298712	Viola
00298708	Trumpet	00298713	Cello

Disney Movie Hits
12 songs
00841420	Flute	00841424	Horn
00841687	Oboe	00841425	Trombone
00841421	Clarinet	00841426	Violin
00841422	Alto Sax	00841427	Viola
00841686	Tenor Sax	00841428	Cello
00841423	Trumpet		

Prices, contents, and availability subject to change without notice.

Disney characters and artwork ™ & © 2021 Disney

Disney Solos
12 songs
00841404	Flute	00841506	Oboe
00841406	Alto Sax	00841409	Trumpet
00841407	Horn	00841410	Violin
00841411	Viola	00841412	Cello
00841405	Clarinet/Tenor Sax		
00841408	Trombone/Baritone		
00841553	Mallet Percussion		

Dixieland Favorites
15 songs
00268756	Flute	0068759	Trumpet
00268757	Clarinet	00268760	Trombone
00268758	Alto Sax		

Billie Eilish
9 songs
00345648	Flute	00345653	Horn
00345649	Clarinet	00345654	Trombone
00345650	Alto Sax	00345655	Violin
00345651	Tenor Sax	00345656	Viola
00345652	Trumpet	00345657	Cello

Favorite Movie Themes
13 songs
00841166	Flute	00841168	Trumpet
00841167	Clarinet	00841170	Trombone
00841169	Alto Sax	00841296	Violin

Gospel Hymns
15 songs
00194648	Flute	00194654	Trombone
00194649	Clarinet	00194655	Violin
00194650	Alto Sax	00194656	Viola
00194651	Tenor Sax	00194657	Cello
00194652	Trumpet		

Great Classical Themes
15 songs
00292727	Flute	00292733	Horn
00292728	Clarinet	00292735	Trombone
00292729	Alto Sax	00292736	Violin
00292730	Tenor Sax	00292737	Viola
00292732	Trumpet	00292738	Cello

The Greatest Showman
8 songs
00277389	Flute	00277394	Horn
00277390	Clarinet	00277395	Trombone
00277391	Alto Sax	00277396	Violin
00277392	Tenor Sax	00277397	Viola
00277393	Trumpet	00277398	Cello

Irish Favorites
31 songs
00842489	Flute	00842495	Trombone
00842490	Clarinet	00842496	Violin
00842491	Alto Sax	00842497	Viola
00842493	Trumpet	00842498	Cello
00842494	Horn		

Michael Jackson
11 songs
00119495	Flute	00119499	Trumpet
00119496	Clarinet	00119501	Trombone
00119497	Alto Sax	00119503	Violin
00119498	Tenor Sax	00119502	Accomp.

Jazz & Blues
14 songs
00841438	Flute	00841441	Trumpet
00841439	Clarinet	00841443	Trombone
00841440	Alto Sax	00841444	Violin
00841442	Tenor Sax		

Jazz Classics
12 songs
00151812	Flute	00151816	Trumpet
00151813	Clarinet	00151818	Trombone
00151814	Alto Sax	00151819	Violin
00151815	Tenor Sax	00151821	Cello

Les Misérables
13 songs
00842292	Flute	00842297	Horn
00842293	Clarinet	00842298	Trombone
00842294	Alto Sax	00842299	Violin
00842295	Tenor Sax	00842300	Viola
00842296	Trumpet	00842301	Cello

Metallica
12 songs
02501327	Flute	02502454	Horn
02501339	Clarinet	02501329	Trombone
02501332	Alto Sax	02501334	Violin
02501333	Tenor Sax	02501335	Viola
02501330	Trumpet	02501338	Cello

Motown Classics
15 songs
00842572	Flute	00842576	Trumpet
00842573	Clarinet	00842578	Trombone
00842574	Alto Sax	00842579	Violin
00842575	Tenor Sax		

Pirates of the Caribbean
16 songs
00842183	Flute	00842188	Horn
00842184	Clarinet	00842189	Trombone
00842185	Alto Sax	00842190	Violin
00842186	Tenor Sax	00842191	Viola
00842187	Trumpet	00842192	Cello

Queen
17 songs
00285402	Flute	00285407	Horn
00285403	Clarinet	00285408	Trombone
00285404	Alto Sax	00285409	Violin
00285405	Tenor Sax	00285410	Viola
00285406	Trumpet	00285411	Cello

Simple Songs
14 songs
00249081	Flute	00249087	Horn
00249093	Oboe	00249089	Trombone
00249082	Clarinet	00249090	Violin
00249083	Alto Sax	00249091	Viola
00249084	Tenor Sax	00249092	Cello
00249086	Trumpet	00249094	Mallets

Superhero Themes
14 songs
00363195	Flute	00363200	Horn
00363196	Clarinet	00363201	Trombone
00363197	Alto Sax	00363202	Violin
00363198	Tenor Sax	00363203	Viola
00363199	Trumpet	00363204	Cello

Star Wars
16 songs
00350900	Flute	00350907	Horn
00350913	Oboe	00350908	Trombone
00350903	Clarinet	00350909	Violin
00350904	Alto Sax	00350910	Viola
00350905	Tenor Sax	00350911	Cello
00350906	Trumpet	00350914	Mallet

Taylor Swift
15 songs
00842532	Flute	00842537	Horn
00842533	Clarinet	00842538	Trombone
00842534	Alto Sax	00842539	Violin
00842535	Tenor Sax	00842540	Viola
00842536	Trumpet	00842541	Cello

Video Game Music
13 songs
00283877	Flute	00283883	Horn
00283878	Clarinet	00283884	Trombone
00283879	Alto Sax	00283885	Violin
00283880	Tenor Sax	00283886	Viola
00283882	Trumpet	00283887	Cello

Wicked
13 songs
00842236	Flute	00842241	Horn
00842237	Clarinet	00842242	Trombone
00842238	Alto Sax	00842243	Violin
00842239	Tenor Sax	00842244	Viola
00842240	Trumpet	00842245	Cello

HAL·LEONARD®

0122
488

101 SONGS

BIG COLLECTIONS OF FAVORITE SONGS ARRANGED FOR SOLO INSTRUMENTALISTS.

101 BROADWAY SONGS

00154199 Flute...............$15.99
00154200 Clarinet.......$15.99
00154201 Alto Sax........$15.99
00154202 Tenor Sax....$16.99
00154203 Trumpet.......$15.99
00154204 Horn.............$15.99
00154205 Trombone...$15.99
00154206 Violin...........$15.99
00154207 Viola...$15.99
00154208 Cello...$15.99

101 DISNEY SONGS

00244104 Flute.............$17.99
00244106 Clarinet.......$17.99
00244107 Alto Sax........$17.99
00244108 Tenor Sax...$17.99
00244109 Trumpet.......$17.99
00244112 Horn.............$17.99
00244120 Trombone...$17.99
00244121 Violin.............$17.99
00244125 Viola...$17.99
00244126 Cello...$17.99

101 MOVIE HITS

00158087 Flute.............$15.
00158088 Clarinet.......$15.
00158089 Alto Sax......$15.
00158090 Tenor Sax...$15.
00158091 Trumpet........$15.
00158092 Horn.............$15.
00158093 Trombone...$15.
00158094 Violin...........$15.
00158095 Viola...$15.
00158096 Cello...$15.

101 CHRISTMAS SONGS

00278637 Flute.............$15.99
00278638 Clarinet.......$15.99
00278639 Alto Sax......$15.99
00278640 Tenor Sax.$15.99
00278641 Trumpet........$15.99
00278642 Horn.............$14.99
00278643 Trombone...$15.99
00278644 Violin...........$15.99
00278645 Viola...$15.99
00278646 Cello...$15.99

101 HIT SONGS

00194561 Flute..............$17.99
00197182 Clarinet.........$17.99
00197183 Alto Sax........$17.99
00197184 Tenor Sax.....$17.99
00197185 Trumpet.........$17.99
00197186 Horn..............$17.99
00197187 Trombone.....$17.99
00197188 Violin.............$17.99
00197189 Viola...$17.99
00197190 Cello...$17.99

101 POPULAR SONGS

00224722 Flute.............$17.
00224723 Clarinet.......$17.
00224724 Alto Sax......$17.
00224725 Tenor Sax...$17.
00224726 Trumpet.......$17.
00224727 Horn.............$17.
00224728 Trombone...$17.
00224729 Violin............$17.
00224730 Viola...$17.
00224731 Cello...$17.

101 CLASSICAL THEMES

00155315 Flute.............$15.99
00155317 Clarinet.........$15.99
00155318 Alto Sax........$15.99
00155319 Tenor Sax.....$15.99
00155320 Trumpet.......$15.99
00155321 Horn.............$15.99
00155322 Trombone...$15.99
00155323 Violin...........$15.99
00155324 Viola...$15.99
00155325 Cello...$15.99

101 JAZZ SONGS

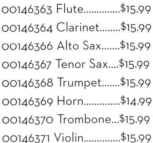

00146363 Flute..............$15.99
00146364 Clarinet........$15.99
00146366 Alto Sax.......$15.99
00146367 Tenor Sax....$15.99
00146368 Trumpet.......$15.99
00146369 Horn.............$14.99
00146370 Trombone...$15.99
00146371 Violin............$15.99
00146372 Viola...$15.99
00146373 Cello...$15.99

101 MOST BEAUTIFUL SONG

00291023 Flute.............$16.
00291041 Clarinet.........$16.
00291042 Alto Sax........$17.
00291043 Tenor Sax...$17.
00291044 Trumpet.......$16.
00291045 Horn.............$16.
00291046 Trombone...$16.
00291047 Violin...........$16.
00291048 Viola...$16.
00291049 Cello...$17.

See complete song lists and sample pages at www.halleonard.com

HAL•LEONARD®
www.halleonard.com

Prices, contents and availability subject to change without notice.